MY ACHY BODY

LIZA FROMER AND FRANCINE GERSTEIN MD

Illustrated by Joe Weissmann

TUNDRA BOOKS

Published in Canada by Tundra Books,
75 Sherbourne Street, Toronto, Ontario M5A 2P9

Published in the United States by Tundra Books of Northern New York,
P.O. Box 1030, Plattsburgh, New York 12901

Library of Congress Control Number: 2010940337

Library and Archives Canada Cataloguing in Publication

Fromer, Liza
　My achy body / Liza Fromer and Francine Gerstein ; illustrated by Joe Weissmann.

(Body works)
ISBN 978-1-77049-204-2　　0874

　1. Human body – Juvenile literature.　2. Human physiology – Juvenile
literature.　3. Human anatomy – Juvenile literature.
I. Gerstein, Francine　II. Weissmann, Joe, 1947-　III. Title.
IV. Series: Body works (Toronto, Ont.)

QP37.F762 2011　　　　　　　j612　　　　　　C2010-907304-5

We acknowledge the financial support of the Government of Canada through the Book
Publishing Industry Development Program (BPIDP) and that of the Government of Ontario
through the Ontario Media Development Corporation's Ontario Book Initiative.
We further acknowledge the support of the Canada Council for the Arts and the Ontario
Arts Council for our publishing program.

ONTARIO ARTS COUNCIL
CONSEIL DES ARTS DE L'ONTARIO

Medium: watercolor on paper

Design: Leah Springate

Printed and bound in China

1 2 3 4 5 6　　　　　　16 15 14 13 12 11

Also available in this Body Works series by Liza Fromer and Francine Gerstein MD, illustrated by Joe Weissmann

Authors' Note

The information in this book is to help you understand your body and learn why it works the way it does.

It's important that you see your family doctor at least once each year. If you're worried about your health or think you might be sick, speak to an adult and see your doctor.

We know that parts of your body can get achy, but what exactly is an ache? An ache is a form of pain. Pain can be physical, or it can be emotional. If you've ever fallen off your bike and scraped your knee, we bet you felt physical pain. You probably felt emotional pain when someone hurt your feelings. You might say emotional pain gives you an ache in your heart. The good news is, both kinds of pain usually get better with time.

Physical pain isn't there to hurt you, but to keep you safe. Pain activates your body's defense system by triggering a reflex reaction. Think of it this way … if you accidentally touch something hot or prickly, you automatically pull your hand away. This reflex reaction helps to make sure you don't do any serious damage to your hand. So how does your body know how to do this when it seems like you're not even telling it to? (Who's in charge here anyway!)

Your body has pain receptors that send signals along your nerves to the spinal cord and up to your brain. Sounds like a long trip, but it actually happens in milliseconds. When the pain signal reaches your spinal cord, the signal is immediately sent back along your motor nerves to

the original site of the pain (for example, the knee you scraped falling off your bike), triggering the muscles to contract. The pain signal is also sent to the brain, but it takes longer to get there (it is farther away). That's why you automatically pull away from painful things before your brain realizes that something has happened!

By the way. . .
When you see MT in this book, it stands for Medical Term.

BRUISES

Bruises (MT: ecchymoses) are discolorations in or below your skin that can look black, blue, and purple. They happen when you bang yourself hard enough to break a blood vessel and blood leaks from the damaged vessel into the surrounding tissue.

It can ache to use that part of your body. For example, if you bruise your leg, it may hurt when you run; and if you bang your toe, it may hurt to put on your shoe. Listen to your body and be gentle with your bruised part, so it can heal.

As the bruise heals, it turns a greenish yellow color while the blood that leaked is absorbed back into your body. When the bruise has healed, your skin returns to its normal color. Now you can put on your shoes and run around again.

If you drop an apple or a banana on the floor, it will bruise too. Be careful with your fruit!

Doctor says:

"If you apply a cool compress with firm pressure right after you bang yourself, your bruise might not be so bad."

SCRAPES

Scrapes (MT: abrasions) are skin wounds that happen when you rub or tear off skin. They're different from cuts because they're not very deep, but they can remove several thin layers of skin and usually come with a little bleeding.

Scrapes can occur on any part of the body, but you usually get them when you fall on your hands, knees, shins, or elbows – especially when you're wearing shorts and a T-shirt! Even though scrapes aren't as deep as cuts, they are often more painful because they affect a larger area of skin and more of your nerve endings.

Since most scrapes are caused by accidents or falls, here are a few tips that could help you avoid them: Pay attention to what you are doing; make sure you know how to use whatever it is that you're using, whether it's a scooter or a two-wheeled bike; always wear protective gear, such as a helmet and pads, for your hands, wrists, elbows, and knees, during sports or recreational activities.

Doctor says:

"If you've just scraped your shin on the sidewalk, your shin is probably dirty. It's important to rinse the scrape with clean water right away. And if you're planning on heading back out to play, it's a good idea to cover the scrape to keep out any more dirt."

SCABS

Not long after you get a cut or a scrape, a reddish brown crust called a scab (MT: sanguineous crust) forms. How does this happen and why do you need scabs? Scabs prevent you from losing too much blood and keep you from getting an infection. You definitely don't want an infection because that would make your body ache.

In your blood, there are three types of blood cells floating around in a liquid (MT: plasma) that help your body make scabs: red blood cells, white blood cells, and platelets. Red blood cells carry oxygen to all the parts of your body. White blood

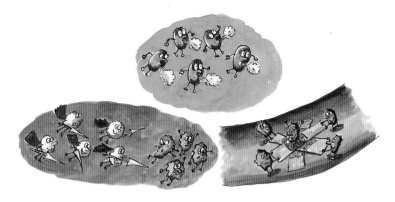

cells help you fight infections. Platelets are the emergency crew that takes care of your scrapes and cuts by making sure your blood sticks together (MT: clots) to form a plug that stops any bleeding.

Protein is also found in plasma, which creates small strings that tie everything together – the final step in building a strong scab. Scabs protect your wound until new skin forms underneath.

True or False?

The world's biggest scab collection belongs to Steve "Crusty" Smith from Moose Jaw, Saskatchewan. (*False*. Collecting scabs is totally gross!)

Doctor says:

"It's important not to pick your scabs because you'll damage the skin underneath, which may turn into a scar."

BROKEN BONES

Broken bones (MT: fractures) are common in childhood, and they usually happen during sports or play. Most fractures occur in the wrists and arms because when you fall, your reflex reaction is to put your hands out, to stop yourself from landing on your face. Some breaks are more obvious than others, but if you hear a snap or grinding when you fall; if you feel pain, swelling, tenderness, and bruising; or something just doesn't look right, all of these are clues that you may have broken a bone.

When you're young, your bones are different from the bones of an adult, so the fractures you get will differ too. Your bones are slightly bendable, so you'll get fractures that mostly happen just to kids. For example, a greenstick fracture is when a bone breaks only on one side, like a new branch growing on a tree – it will bend a bit, but it won't snap in half. An older twig would likely snap completely in two.

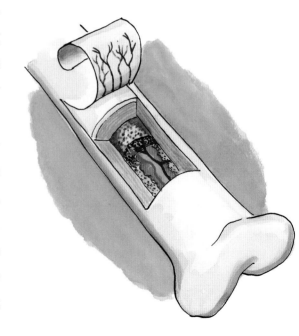

Your fractures are also treated differently than an adult's because your bones heal faster. Other tissues like skin and muscle heal themselves with scar tissue, but bone is different because it heals itself with actual bone! There are two ongoing processes in your bones throughout your life: bone-building and bone-removing. Bone-building cells are called osteoblasts and bone-removing cells are called osteoclasts. Your osteoblasts are more active than an adult's because you are growing, so your bones heal faster. Kids' bones also have special parts called growth plates (the areas of your bone that are responsible for growing).

If you break a bone, see a doctor right away. You'll need a cast or splint to keep the bone still and allow it to heal. A cast is made of two layers: a hard shell of plaster or fiberglass that prevents the broken bone from moving and a soft inside layer for skin comfort. A splint is like a half cast that is wrapped with an elastic bandage to ensure the fractured bone stays in place. Bones take many weeks to heal, depending on the bone and the age and health of the person with the fracture.

#1 The smallest bone in your body is the stirrup bone (MT: stapes), deep in your ear.

#2 The largest bone in your body is the thigh bone (MT: femur).

True or False?

Arm bones heal faster than leg bones. (*True.* Your leg bones take longer to heal because they support the entire weight of your body.)

Doctor says:

"Even our hard and strong bones are made of approximately one-quarter water."

SPRAINS AND STRAINS

Your bones are held together by strong bands of tissue called ligaments. A sprain is a ligament injury caused by suddenly twisting or turning a joint out of its normal position. But there are other important players on this team. You also have tendons, which connect your muscles to your bones. A strain is an injury to a muscle or a tendon, and it is caused by overusing, forcing, or overstretching your muscles or tendons.

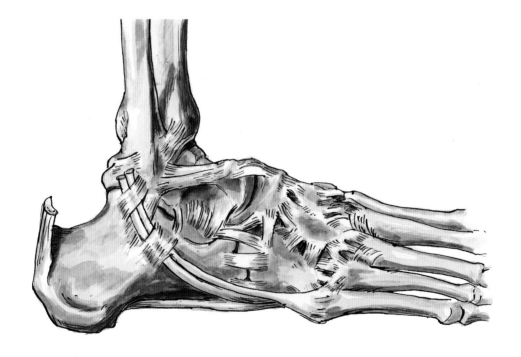

Unlike fractures, sprains and strains are not common in children. That's because the growth plates in your bones aren't as strong as your muscles, tendons, and ligaments, so you're more likely to get a break than a sprain or strain. Symptoms of a sprain or strain are pain, swelling, redness, bruising, and difficulty using the injured part of your body. For example, if you sprain your ankle, you may walk with a limp. Sometimes it's difficult to tell whether you have a sprain, strain, or fracture because the symptoms can be similar. It's best to see a doctor so that he or she can figure it out!

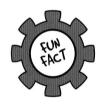

FUN FACT The most commonly sprained parts of the body are the ankles, knees, and wrists.

True or False?
Dogs can get sprains too. (*True.*)

Doctor says:
"If you have a sprain or a strain, it's important to rest the injured area so it will have a chance to heal."

STOMACH ACHES

If you've ever had a stomach ache (MT: abdominal pain), you're definitely not alone – most children get one from time to time. Stomach aches are caused by lots of different things, including stomach flu, migraines, appendicitis, or eating too much!

Even when your parents and your doctor are sure that nothing is wrong with your health, it's still possible for you to have a stomach ache. But this kind of ache is probably an emotional one, like the kind we talked about at the beginning of this book. You may have a stomach ache when you're worried about something, like the first day of school, a big test, or when your feelings are hurt. If you're worried, it will help if you talk about it with an adult.

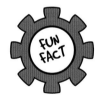

Stomach aches are one of the most common reasons that children see their doctor.

True or False?

A 150-pound marathon runner can have the same size stomach as a 300-pound sumo wrestler. (*True*. Overweight people often have the same size stomachs as people of normal weight.)

EARACHES

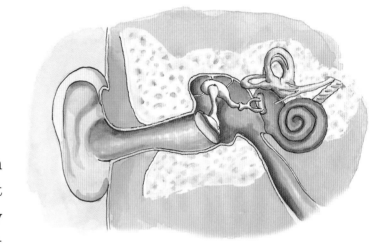

Have you ever noticed that when you get a cold, you sometimes get an earache too? There are many different causes of earaches, but one common cause is an ear infection – especially in children.

Your ears have three parts: the outer, middle, and inner ear. A tube (MT: Eustachian tube) connects the middle ear to the back of the nose and throat. This tube keeps your middle ear clear, but when you get a cold and your nose is congested, the tube can swell up. Mucus from the back of your nose gets into the tube, and bacteria can grow. This yucky combination increases the pressure behind the eardrum and causes ear pain.

If you have an earache, your doctor can look into your ear with a special instrument (MT: otoscope) to see what's causing it. Sometimes you need medicine to help your earache go away; sometimes it gets better on its own.

Doctor says:

"You can't get an ear infection from playing outside in the cold, but you can get an earache. The cold weather can cause a pressure change in your ear that some people find painful. One easy way to help prevent this is by wearing a warm hat or earmuffs."

SORE THROATS

You can get a sore throat (MT: pharyngitis) from many things, including allergens or dry air, but they are mostly caused by infections from the same viruses that cause colds or flu. Viruses are tiny germs that cause infections. They enter your body through your mouth, nose, or eyes. So how do they manage to get in there? One easy way is if someone coughs or sneezes into the open air around you and you breathe it in. These germs spread easily – sometimes all you have to do is touch an object (such as a toy, a telephone, or a doorknob) that someone with a cold has touched and then wipe your mouth, nose, or eyes.

If your throat hurts, your parents may take you to the doctor for a checkup. The doctor might use the otoscope to get a better look at your throat. If you open your mouth wide and say "*ahhh*," the doctor will have an even better view. Just like earaches, sometimes the doctor will give you medicine to help your sore throat get better; other times it gets better on its own.

True or False?

Because a giraffe has such a long neck, it can get sore throats in different spots all at the same time. (*False.* A giraffe may have a long neck, but it has only one throat.)

Doctor says:

"It's always a good idea to cough or sneeze into your sleeve if you don't have a tissue. Washing your hands is also important. A good scrub will help you rinse the germs right down the drain. You should also keep your hands away from your mouth, nose, and eyes."

Isn't it amazing what your achy body can do!

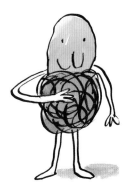

Glossary

Allergens, compress, fiberglass, infection, millisecond, plaster, protein, receptors (sensory), reflex, spinal cord.

Allergens: Substances that cause allergic reactions in people.

Compress: A soft pad applied with pressure to a part of the body to supply heat, cold, moisture, or medication to help with pain, swelling, or infection.

Fiberglass: A material containing tiny glass fibers.

Infection: Occurs when organisms cause sickness in other living things.

Millisecond: One-thousandth of a second.

Plaster: A protective mixture that hardens when it dries.

Protein: An organic compound that is an essential part of your body and its cells.

Receptors (sensory): Special parts of nerves that react to things like touch, pain, and temperature.

Reflex: An automatic response to a stimulus (e.g., pain, heat) by your nervous system.

Spinal cord: A ropelike structure of nerve tissue that runs from the bottom of your brain down your vertebral canal, sending motor and sensory messages to and from your brain.